Barry World

By Barry F. Thomas

DORRANCE PUBLISHING CO
EST. 1920
PITTSBURGH, PENNSYLVANIA 15238

Dorrance Publishing Co
585 Alpha Drive
Suite 103
Pittsburgh, PA 15238
Visit our website at *www.dorrancebookstore.com*

ISBN: 979-8-8872-9026-3
eISBN: 979-8-8872-9526-8

Me

Glasses are being poured, hands are being shaken. Paper being punched, somebody is lifting a box and have nothing to do with it...since I was laid off months ago...I am nothing. It wasn't the greatest job...but it was something. We had a great camaraderie at work. Well, thank God I got a year of severance, if not Maggie and I would have hit hard times. Right now times are hard in my head. My back pains are sporadic as are my thoughts of suicide!

Country Time

Back at the country place, my parents and two sisters were away. I was five years old and just discovered my first 1970s-era *Playboy*. I leafed through the pages, my excitement growing along with my little pecker. This was heaven...all mine. The only other time I can remember being aroused back then was in the first grade. My French teacher leaned in and I looked down her top. When I saw those sweet breasts dangling, I knew what I wanted. Upon finishing the magazine, I realized they would be home soon. Oh! What was that? It seemed I'd shit myself. So off to the woods to fling my soiled underwear deep into the forgiving woods, then back inside to clean up...perfect.

Coke Floats

When I was a kid, on Saturdays it felt as if we were all a happy family. It was the simplest thing. My dad would take scoops of vanilla ice cream and plop them into glasses full of Coke. Coke Floats, as he would call them. I would call it Happiness. Our family being happy together.

Walt Disney World

It was the late seventies, August 16th, a day before my birthday. Elvis had died. We were in the South so the country was mourning. We went on to Disney World anyways. We stayed at the Spartan Inn, it was not very memorable but comfy. The park was perfection for a kid my age. I'm not kidding when I say that everything was magical. The Haunted Mansion was a hoot. The daily parade was sublime. "It's a Small World" was fantastic. The ultimate thing was "Space Mountain," a rollercoaster in the dark. Heavy!!

Comics

As I grew up, I collected comic books. I would wait patiently for the new issues to come out. I would read them once and then place them into the mylar plastic pouches. My friends and I were nerds, not like the ones you see on the television that have all this coolness. We were big nerds.

Ages 6 and Up

I have lovely memories of my grandmother. When I was a kid, my grandparents came all the way from South Carolina at Christmas. There were so many presents you could barely walk around. Nanny is what we called her, she was the most affectionate person I have ever known. She would give these bear hugs and swing you around. My granddad, on the other hand, was the coldest person you could ever meet. We all went out for Chinese food and after it was all over, I tried hugging him. He pushed me away, saying, "We don't do that! Jerk!"

I would say that there are some awkward years to follow. Thinking and only thinking about girls and yet too *peureux* to approach them. Going through school, I would not feel comfortable so my mother would scribble "Not feeling well!" on a piece of paper and that would be it. It was comic books that ruled the day. Captain Marvel was my favorite... misunderstood... but Marvel comics were not quite the juggernaut they are today. At ten years old, though summers were always the best, going to the local pool was always a child's way of lounging, watching Chantal, the older, well-breasted lifeguard. We would jump off the high diving board professing my love for her. I thought my childhood was not so bad and then it happened. Dean was my best friend...a childhood friend...but when his older brother was alone with me it was a nightmare. He did some things, some I remember, some I can't, and some flash like pictures when I can't sleep. My head pushed down, I can still feel a burning, bloating and searing sensation...wanting it to be over. I couldn't feel my legs. Fear multiplied within me. He was in his twenties. I can always remember his stubble against me. I always felt as though I let it happen. God help me, Mom. And in more awkward years there was fucking.

Sports

There was a constant push and it was ever present. First came hockey and later there was soccer. I swear to you, I sucked at both. I always felt my father's disappointment, but it left me feeling as if "If I can't do it, then don't do it." I have never given a toss about any sport or any franchise, you know, and I don't give a fuck!!!!!

I was just a little guy in elementary school. I had a favorite shirt. It was my light blue shirt. It seemed every day I wore it, the day would always turn out good. No one would pick on me. Once I was late for a school trip to Ottawa and barely made it before the bus left. On the halfway mark we stopped for lunch…I had no lunch…I had some licorice…Peter V. offered me a chocolate bar for all of my licorice. Done! I gave him my stuff and got nothing in return. He just laughed. People like to laugh and sometimes a blue shirt just doesn't cut it, baby.

I was in grade four and was clowning around in music class, as I had been anointed the new class clown. My teacher, Mrs. Sheath, had had enough of my antics and dragged me into the hallway. She gave me such a slap across my face that I can still feel it today. Yet all I could feel that day was shame.

My Teens

Reached my early teens, I discovered something new…HELLO, ALCOHOL! All the older kids with their lumberjackets were drinking in a wooded area near my house. I was already beginning to smoke but this was something else. I was on the way back from a Scout meeting and thought I would infiltrate this degenerate society. I knew someone there so I was feeling cocky. An older girl named Wendy was there, beer in hand. She was much taller than me with long brown hair and freckles. Not terribly attractive. I didn't feel nervous.

"Wanna sip?" she asked.

"Sure," I answered and took a few generous slugs of the not-so-cold Brador that had been offered. The once-full beer was now empty. I knew now I felt as if I could ask one of the other kids for a smoke, which I did.

Wendy was amazed a little kid like me could drink like that. She tapped me on the shoulder as I put out my cigarette as manly as possible.

"More?" she asked. And she handed me another Brador.

Down it went. I walked home with a worried mind, under the light of a silvery moon. But my parents never suspected a thing. When I went to bed, I had this great sensation in my body and mind. This was the way I always wanted to feel...so nice...but never would....

The feeling of my mother cradling me before school on a snowy grade-2 morning. Feeling that for one brief moment was just one component of drinking. My next drinking experiment happened soon after. Within the same month. Again, I was coming home from the Scouts and there was a chill in the air, ran into Steven, my neighbor. He was always ahead in terms of what was cool. We went to his place and eventually got into a bottle of white rum. We laughed as we drunkenly threw Christmas ornaments at one another. Until his mother got home and I was unceremoniously paraded out the door.

My problems were just beginning. I was stinking drunk. When I not-so-gingerly came inside I was having problems getting my boots off. My parents were in the other room watching THE DONNY & MARIE OSMOND SPECIAL. That alone should have tipped me off that I was in hell...but no! When I was discovered there in the kitchen waving I was taken away and given a beating...compliments of DAD.

Then my mother sent me off to school the next day severely hungover. I thought I learned a lesson there but alcohol would come back in my life again. One day, it would result in a degradation trip, but not now. One day, I would be innocently riding my ten-speed in gym shorts, the next in the bushes drinking beer or cider, whatever I could get. A mix of hedonism and innocence so young.

One night, a plethora and I biked to Saint Helen's Island, just off the Jacques Cartier Bridge. The night went like this...mayhem and chaos on BMX bikes. I had no bike but I was driven on the handlebars of a friend. We spread general mayhem, just silly shit, hurting no one. When the night was over, I was left alone, no lift home. I began walking home over the bridge. Toward the end, I straddled the side of the bridge. I saw all the cars whizzing by. Why wouldn't anyone stop? To this day, I still find myself hanging off the edge of the bridge.

Cindy, My Sister

Toxic, that was what she was. Even as children she was toxic. She was so jealous of her baby brother. It would manifest in different ways. "Why did he get that?" she would complain.

Plain aggression and even a sexual liaison...AWFUL!

When my father got sick, she was there. After my father died, his baseball team decided to have a memorial for him and she was there too. I sat next to her at the memorial. She said to me, "I'm done with this family!" and she was. It was okay with me if I didn't see her again. What bothered me the most was the fact that in the past ten years she had not gone to visit her mother or even called her for Mother's Day, her birthday or for Christmas. Instead she visited her aunt, my mother's sister. She told her all these lies about how she was being treated by her family but she neglected to tell her about what she had done wrong.

To Rock...

With the eighties beginning, I happened upon an album. It was black. The record was *Back in Black* by AC/DC, can't remember where I got it, only that I loved it. The guitars along with everything else got me. I knew then that this was a lifelong thing. I would play it constantly despite my father's disapproval. A couple of years later, I heard Steven pumping something new out of his little boombox. We were attempting to get drunk behind a grocery store in some bushes. The band was Judas Priest. Without a doubt, my favorite band ever. I couldn't figure out why there were two singers. Then I realized the singer was just THAT good. Later he would become known as the metal god! The music made me feel so good. In that time, I didn't know I was bipolar but they made me feel bipolar. This music made me feel like myself. It was like I had had a new identity and it was rockin'. The polar opposite to my meek and mild personality. I was always small for my age, which caused a lot of problems in the girl department for Little Barry. We would be in a circle of teens going around telling our ages and when it got to me I would say FIFTEEN and everyone would laugh. "You look like you're ten!!" one of the meaner kids would say.

1986

Beavis!!!! So not only did we indulge in hash, pot and beer, there was also PAM...correct...in a spray can. We would spray it in a sandwich bag and inhale. I have never had such visions...hyper realistic.

I saw my boy, Rob, as a Transformer taxi cab. One guy was convinced he had a spinning chicken on his head. Once hallucinated I was in the Arctic, fending off angry seals with a pelt. When it wore off, I was hitting my friends with a PAM bag. Rob and I spent the summer in Steven's cat-piss-smelling basement listening to Judas Priest's *Turbo* album. Rob, the ginger, had become a good friend. I would honestly say we were the Beavis and Butthead of the eighties...heh-heh. Back to the basement.

Steven's older brother would be upstairs watching *Top Gun* with his jock buddies. We were more interested in *Pee-Wee's Playhouse*. Many times, we went late that summer. Nobody looking at the stars. Scored 2nd-row tickets to Priest. For three friends and myself. The problem was I had appendicitis...ouch. I lay in my hospital bed distraught until my nurse told me when I was getting out. The day of the concert, even though I was a small guy I felt big with anticipation. I phoned my father and he was cool with letting me go. Bought myself a new ticket. When I got there I ran into Steven. He magically made my nosebleed ticket something awesome. There I was lighting my lighter in my feeble sweatpants, not very metal. Oh, well! In a brief setback, I had a bad trip on LSD that year. My buddies and I saw *Back to the Future* one night, after that...WOW...I had a bad trip. Rob would say, "BT stands for bad trip"...whoa. To this day I wonder of the impact. Not long after that there was a band everyone was talking about...METALLICA!!! Fucking loved them. They were straight to the point with music so fast and powerful, you might want to smash something. Especially if you were drunk! The show they put on at the auditorium was incredible. I had never seen so many bikers before or really seen ANY bikers. They were doing blow right in the open on the bar. Cracking skulls. I felt a Thunderdome vibe. There was a vicious fight before they came on. One skinny guy with a mohawk and a larger metal guy.... There was a circle pit around them, making sure the fight continued. One guy turned to the bloodhungry crowd for kudos when the skinny dude went and punched him in the back of the head. To this day, I can still hear that "klok" sound. Security finally did their thing and Metallica killed it!!!

In 1987, my first real job was at the end of the eighties. Dominion Textiles was where my father worked and he got me in. We would drive in together every morning, him with his wisps of hair yet still charming and me with my mullet and Metallica shirt. It was there I met Jerry. He stood there five foot dumb, the hairiest motherfucker I had ever seen, thick glasses and corduroy pants just as thick. A hilarious but wimpy demeanor. The Lebanese answer to Woody Allen. The day he was let go, I thought I would take a chance. I knew he was going over the border in search of some friendly American girls. I asked him if I could tag along. He agreed and we began our weird but good friendship.

The following year would take us to bars, piano bars and wherever there were women. Jerry did well in the bars only because he asked every woman there to dance with him. "0 for 4," he would say. One time, a woman recoiled in horror, giving him the anti-vampire sign. HILARIOUS. One Friday, Jerry had met three girls from Owen Sound, Ontario. He needed some wingmen. I was in and so was Dean. On Saturday, Jerry had promised the girls two good-looking guys. After the night was done, we all went back to the hotel they were staying at. We all made out in the dark until I couldn't take it anymore. Brenda was a big blonde girl who looked great naked. We were both naked when I led her out to hallway. I loved her white body and was just sucking her large tits. I laid her down, spread her legs and began licking. Right there on the carpet. Then I fucked her in every position I could think of. Then we got up, walked away, my cock dripping when I noticed a red V on the carpet. *V for victory,* I thought. She called me a few times later but I couldn't be bothered.

One time we were doing the cross-country thing and ran into a couple of hometown girls. My girl's name was Randy. And randy she was!! We had some great sex. A very nice body with blonde bob cut and freckles. Her pussy was hot to the touch. These type of things would happen from time to time. The last time I would see Jerry was the night we hit the racetrack before hitting the bars. I picked long shots in the first two races and raked in five hundred smackers. Jerry was disgusted. This was beyond jealousy. Why couldn't he be happy for me? I would have been happy for him. He wouldn't even speak to me the rest of the night. I never saw him after that.

The 90s Redux

Vancouver wasn't my first choice for a change in life but it was, in fact, Hammer Time. Had some friends out there who had a small spare bedroom in the house they resided in. The unseen paradox of cohabitation is in itself a paradox. I lived with some sweet people and some awful as well. Some (the brothers) worked at the hospital. "Hey! See fucking doctors every day!" It was almost like the Old West...everybody staking out their claim. Due to the in-house friction caused by the only female there, I only lasted a year. She was dubbed the squash and was going out with the alpha male. Or so he thought...endless blow-ups. While I was there, I had a few different jobs...driver, dishwasher, clerk. Nothing seemed to work for me. When I was a driver, I got lost all the time. When I was a clerk, I had a memory problem. When I was a dishwasher, I was awful. Time to go home. I returned home with the sound of grunge ringing in my ears and I liked it. I was still a heavy metal maniac but I welcomed new kinds of music now. I even developed an affinity for the old-school country music that my parents frequently listened to. But I was bankrupt. Morally, my parents weren't about to kick me out but I could tell that they were getting sick of my welfare scene.

1993

HALLELUIAH!!!! I had gone to a few job interviews and all of them had gone south. And then came the Doheny McKenzie interview. They were a law firm so I won't really be talking about them except to say I've met some tremendously awesome people in my 28 years there. The interview was a snap. Jeanette, head of HR, interviewed me. I made her laugh, she made me laugh. It went great. Halfway through the interview Gail, who would later be my boss, dropped by. She was a little harried but I think she wanted to check out the new guy. We hit it off immediately and it turned out that she would become a lifelong friend. She got me right away...not many people do. God bless the ones who do. Two days later, I got the call to tell me that I was in. It felt fantastic. On the first week, Gail asked me to pick up a mailbag. When I turned about-face there was Gail and her cute friend Maggie, smiling sheepishly. I let out a little "Heh-heh" and they just kept on smiling. Right away I hit it off with a lawyer there, Peter, in maritime law. What a sweet man. He has become a judge now. We still go for beers whenever he is in town. That was when I first met Maggie. She was the most beautiful girl I had ever seen. A short haircut and dyed red, smoky dark brown eyes and the greatest full-figured body you could ever ask for. I felt a strong connection. We would become fast friends, trading books, going to movies and having great in-depth conversations as to what it all really meant. The tipping point was there and it was obvious.

In the late summer, I saw Pearl Jam in concert. They were like nothing I had ever experienced. Eddie looked really upset as he pointed people out and shot laser eyes. It felt totally honest, angry and spiritual. I never had one drink that night. The joint I had was totally mashed. Due to the heat wave, my shirt was off within minutes of arriving and there so were many girls, I slid up to the ginormous mosh pit. The next day something bigger happened, Maggie and I planned to go to dinner. I would tell her all about the concert. We went to a "bring your own wine" Greek restaurant on Prince Arthur. We were seated and everything went fine until I realized something. The chatter in my mind was telling me something. She was the one. For the very first time I thought...*I'M IN LOVE!* Then one of the quasi-homeless persons came by selling roses. I had to do it. Maggie was mortified. I have never seen anyone more uncomfortable. I said goodbye after the wine was long gone.

The next week was a little dicey at work. I would try to say something clever and it would just die. I hadn't counted on the Peel Pub, though. Yes. I would ask her to go. We went the next week and had the instant connection. There were vibes. We constantly caught one another gazing. She drove me home in a weathered but trusty blue Ford Tempo. I gave her a kiss on the cheek before I went in. "It's tradition," I said. I didn't know what the fuck I was talking about! It worked, though, she called me the next day. A couple of weeks later we went out for beers. We also rented a cheap homicide motel, we had marathon sex. I drunkenly looked up at the mirrored ceiling and said, "Get me a shotgun! I'm going to blow my head off!" She brought breakfast the next morning. She would not take my calls the following week but she gave in a week later. I later discovered that when I'm at my happiest and highest I want to end my life even when I am at my lowest. It's still a mystery to me.

(COLLECT ANOTHER MEMORY)

Before we got going on vacation I needed Maggie to meet my parents. We had planned a trip to Vermont. We were at my parents' packing my bags. This would be the very first girl that I had brought home to meet the parents. When my parents showed up, I yelled to Maggie that they had arrived!! She had nowhere to run. I was upstairs but I could hear laughter. If there's one thing, my father was a charming man and in this case disarmingly so. We went on our way to Vermont...Maggie in black suede and me in leather. The most important thing was that it was the middle of the night when I snuggled up to her and said, "I love you!" She said, "I love you too!" We took many black-and-white photos in the woods, me hanging from a tree, her sassing it up impishly...like a wood nymph. When Maggie let me off at home it was in full swing. My sister, Doris, was there with her family. When we came to a full stop, I gave Maggie a soulful kiss for the ages. Then the door swung open and Doris wanted to meet Maggie. She was beyond shy. She sped off and Doris gave chase.... "MAAAGGGI-IEEE!!!" It's hell of a cartoonish moment when I think about it. Doris and Maggie finally met and are fast friends today.

One other rough time for me was Christmas. I would be going to her place for Christmas Eve, which was when her family celebrated Christmas. I drove over the bridge, chugging down multiple beers in my trusty old Cutlass. She hosted fourteen people, which I wasn`t ready for. But I had no fucking choice. When I got there her brother began fucking with me instantly. A couple of other people even joined in. I guess I was the new kid. Halfway through supper I vomited violently. It was terrible. By two in the morning, it was finally over. Torture follows happiness and on and on. I can remember wanting to be near Maggie because I felt so uncomfortable but I didn't like the situation. Except for GAIL, she got me!

Down South

And the South will rise again...sort of...South Carolina. This was the big one!! Before I had my breakdown, I used to do the driving. Pioneering through state after state...finally stopping in Wilkes-Barre, PA. The best feeling in the world was taking a dip in the outdoor pool after a long drive with a "St. Paulie's Girl" six-pack for good measure. Back then, I could stop at six. I began having a liking for the 7/11 stores. They had hotdogs roasting, had hot cheese and chili. Oh, God!!! There I was, outside the 7/11 with the chili dripping down my chin onto my vintage Metallica shirt. I'm not proud...just saying! Then, off we went. We ended up in Mount Pleasant near Charleston. It was great. All the amenities close by, some good restaurants along with grocery stores. We took some Southern day tours...wholly inaccurate, as I would tell Maggie. Those plantations are probably gone now, I'm sure. One night, we ate somewhere called "Sticky Fingers." They took ribs to the next level. I felt like a big fat pig when I loaded myself into the car. Driving back to the room was only a five-minute affair. On this drive, I noticed a sign on the Holiday Inn saying "Karaoke Tonight"...I was intrigued. There were maybe eight people in the bar. Some dude was singing "We're an American Band" terribly. Right away I knew I could do much better. Yeah, wait until they get a load of me! The problem was that I was very nervous. I would stand up ready to hit the stage, then cower back into my chair. After my fifth beer, I said to Maggie, "It's time!" I went up and sang "Breaking the Law."\ It wasn't the greatest rendition but by God, I did it. My first karaoke. Some random local came up to me later and said, "Wow, man...haven't heard that in a while." Cool. That's where my love for karaoke began.

When we returned to the room I was bouncing off the walls. I kept asking Maggie how I did over and over until she blew her stack. Even then, I still felt awesome. My favorite beach memory from that time would be Edisto. It was windy and the surf was rough but it just had this intangible charm. I warned Maggie that we needn't put up a beach umbrella. She was totally noncompliant. Ten minutes later I was running down the beach chasing this damned umbrella. People got a good laugh. Not long after I had my revenge. Maggie was feeling cocky. We had this cheap Styrofoam boogie board on which she went waist deep into the rough water. When she surfed in the water, she was thrashed all about. I can remember her standing there in a daze, tiny rocks all embedded in her bum. God love her. It was now overcast so we were getting ready to leave. Before we did I spied this murder haired girl covered in tattoos. She had a great body and did not care. She dove right into that ocean and swam out.... Wow.

When we were back at my mom's and the weather was pretty nice, Maggie felt so comfortable with my parents that she DEMANDED to mow the lawn. It was eleven-thirty and no one suspected a thing. I opened a Corona. We were still on vacation. I made a half-beer and half-tequila drink. When nobody was looking I took a large sip of my father's rum. Maggie worked as I got wasted. One more shot of my father's rum and I was okay...not okay. I would sneak many more sips in years to come...hidden shots of wine chugs...it went on. But we would always remember our times camping...Maine, Vermont, Massachusetts, South Carolina!!!! Nothing nicer than a Carolina sunset. These would prove to be our best times.

Wreck of the Old '97

At this time, I thought my parents were plotting against me. If that wasn't enough, I would hear "BARRY" in the television. I was on the ragged edge. When I would have a panic attack at work...my God...I felt as if people could see through me, judging me and laughing at me. My face was flush and people noticed. My heart pounded like a bass drum!!!! I wanted to run but I would tell people it was lack of sleep. Work was also a factor. I now had to be part of an army of idiots as our company grew, still I never called in sick and never would. Maggie and I had become distant. I had wanted to live with her for many years. Her father had been diagnosed with Parkinson's disease and she refused to leave him. This would have got a pass if her parents hadn't worshipped the grounds her brother walked on. Or maybe not, but the whole fucking burden of her family was on HER. I felt that Maggie should have been with me. Her sister had nothing going on. Then I lost Maggie and nothing hurt more. Suddenly, I was looking sharp and acting sharper!!! I was pure manic. The bus terminal was in my building and one night it was so backed up that I didn`t know what to do. I did know there was a bistro on the main floor... "La Cucina." I went and ordered a beer. There she was...Samantha...I was smitten with her. Short, dark, spiky hair with a Sandra Bullock thing going on. I would drop in Mondays, Wednesdays, and Thursdays after work, hoping to catch a glimpse of her. Although I was obsessing over Samantha, my stomach was twisting for Maggie. I never stopped loving her. Samantha had begun to express interest in me. We continued on like this for a month. So I would get up for work drunk, pound back three coffees, and off I went. My boss pulled me aside and asked if I was okay.... "Yeah!" I was unaware that my HIGH mood was actually a manic state punctuated by moments of extreme sadness....

I photocopied the definition of HELL from the dictionary one day at work. Enlarged it four hundred percent.... I made copies and plastered them all over my room. I also hammered some Polaroids of Samantha on the wall. This was where my father stepped in...just in time. I woke up crying that day. He and my mother drove me to the Montreal General for psychiatric evaluation. I finally realized that I was sick. My parents left me there and over the span of the night I saw four different doctors. None worse than Dr. Montego. A bald, thin man with a lisp. He said, "Can you still cum?" I thought, *Oh ...you fucking little faggot!* but said nothing. Then it occurred to me that I have repressed memories. It all started to come back to me. The sexual abuse, things I let happen. I felt horrible. The clothes I was wearing should be burned. I should be burned. I kept everything to myself and left the following day on the condition I would attend group therapy. The group was called the Transitional Day Program. It was absolute bullshit. The day would begin as follows: Teacher would say, "What color are you today?" My meds were beige so I said beige. Well, this fat bearded fuck named Barry had something to say. He always did. I wasn't there to fight so I passed on Barry. I would say his name but he seemed the type to sue. At one point we had to pass around a beach ball. When it was turned to Barry he dropped it citing that his left arm didn't work. FUCK YOU, ASSHOLE!!!!!!! Then there was Clive. A bald top with dirty brown hair cascading down. The longest fingernails I've ever seen outside of a movie. Same clothes every time. There was one super-hot chick, though. She knew what I was thinking. FUCK! It never happened. The hospital never followed up with me even when I said enough of this. REUNIFICA-TION. My body was still numb from the medication but I got wholly excited when Maggie called. Things were dead between me and Samantha and I so missed Maggie. Coffee? Absolutely! I met her at Second Cup in Central Station. She looked great. Aside from the heavy awkwardness, things went along fine. Her clothes were dark, her lipstick vermillion. Because I say so. We went to my parents', where I hugged her and said, "I'm sorry for being sick." "Don't," she said. Then we got into a bottle of red wine and began jumping up and down on my bed to the Misfits playing in the background. I missed her. I never knew how much. Although it did not deter my drinking, I knew this was forever.

Maggie and her dad knew I was sick. They took me to St. Joseph's Oratory. There was a long stairway to the chapel. It felt heavy and symbolic. When we finally arrived, I could not believe my eyes. There was Jesus Christ. I was being tried as well. It was a full statue. The cross, the blood, I could not take it. Then Maggie's father handed me a piece of paper. The paper asked, "What do you want?" I took my paper and wrote "love," then put it in the slot. I NEEDED HELP....

Hank

I had been to a lot of concerts. One such concert was Hank Williams III, grandson of troubadour Hank Williams. His music is old-school country and metal. WOW! I went up front and had a beer while Maggie stayed in the wings. As I listened to this hillbilly music I thought of the gay bar we went to before the show. The female bartender hit on Maggie and the gay dude was hating on Maggie for being my fag hag...TOO FUNNY. But now I was heavy into this show. I was standing there just enjoying Hank and then some dude started pushing me over and over...FUCK. I put him in a chokehold and went mental. Then somebody punched me in my jaw. At that point security came and dragged me to the front and asked if I was okay. I bought a beer and watched the rest of the show...HAH! We went home together feeling in love. I just never knew how much. We brought it down just a little and cuddled on the couch. It felt so right, what I had waited for my entire life. I realized then that what I had was incurable...MEDICATION FOREVER. I will enjoy what I can...NICE ICE, BABY. The moon hung over me like a cobalt blue nickel. I wondered why I was bipolar. I was me. I was different.

During the '98 ice storm, I was sleeping in a parka. Everything was iced over...my blue '89 Sentra, the barbeque. The week before I had made a spaghetti sauce, I was not going to let it go to waste. So as I chopped away at the Q I realized what I had to do. I would fire it up and make some noodles and sauce. My neighbours especially appreciated this. They were over the moon. Later I brought out my radio and we sang along to some good old country music, by candlelight, of course. There was a quiet that came over everything never since heard, very special.

Christmas in Charleston

A week in the Extended Stay, the temperatures were freezing. We each went out separately to Christmas shop. This would be our first Christmas alone. I had this great recycling chair. Our hopscotch Christmas had paid off. We were both happy. Maggie even made a little turkey breast with fixin's. Perfect! The next day we walked around Charleston checking out the historic buildings in our brand-new sweaters. We hugged each other hard. We were there.... ABBEY '99, Belfast, Maine. It was bone-chilling cold. We had arrived at a charming little motel off the frozen Eastern Coast on New Year's Eve. The town turned exponential, sleigh rides, high school dances, bake sales, hot chocolate. Still had my beer buzz, though. The musical performances were great. I had been drinking all day. And sometimes the local talent was the shit. I was dreaming. Dreaming was not the hellish nightmare it is now.... I could feel something holding my hand. Oh my God, it was a dog. I awoke to find a dog gnawing on my hand. Her name was Abbey and she was the sweetest thing. A patchy black-and-white pointer. You had to love her. The owners let her roam free. This was her motel. She was a rescue and her previous owners had broken her legs. Nothing really upsets me more.... I feel like I don't care what happens to me, just please don't hurt an animal. My parents joined us New Year's Day. There's video of my dad and me singing George Jones' "Out There Somewhere." I felt closer to him than ever. Not the guy who would fly off the handle, but a friend. 1999 had passed to 2000 and nothing had gone wrong. Eleven A.M. the next day, four beers deep. Something was wrong, I didn't know what.

2000

I would say that it was the dawning of a new time but I found it rather flat. Days bled into others and breakfast was just breakfast. My depression remained a constant. Sometimes not being able to taste food, I learned here to be open about it. Even when some people did not understand like my sister, "Aww, Barr...turn the page!"

Thanks...really!?! Sometimes people would say that everybody has a bad day but when it's seven hundred days, what can you do, stay sexy?!? We got in our car and Abbey sniffed us out. When we pulled out, Abbey chased us. I still had a dog at home. She was a schnauzer shiatzu mix...nineteen pounds of pure love. The most soulful eyes you could imagine, a mix of brown and auburn hair, the classic underbite. She wasn't just cute, she was beyond cute. Sometimes on a walk, she would pick up a gigantic branch and carry it. She would walk along with this thing teetering, people would get such a kick out of this. All of this to say she was a real lady.

Breakdown Again

My second breakdown went as such. I stayed home from work because I was not able to handle it. I had a bottle of Ativan pills. I started popping them one by one. I looked down at Abbey with her beautiful eyes. I couldn't do it. I went to the hospital by ambulance. I went in saying that I had taken pills. I waited an hour to be seen. Through it all, I ended up getting a new doctor with new medication...LITHIUM, which I am still taking today. Going back to work was rough because I had been off on medical leave for a while. I felt shattered. Because of the lithium, my hands shook a lot. My hands would get burned often because of the hot coffee spilling all over my hands.

There was a secretary who knew what had happened to me. Whenever she saw me, she would constantly say, "How was your vacation?"

If I had had cancer, people would have been sympathetic and supportive. Since you can't see my illness, many don't understand that being bipolar can be a life-threatening illness.

9/11

I was someone else living within me. Obviously the Twin Towers tragedy....
Swing low...terrible. That same day Maggie's father was taken to a resi-
dential home. It was where he needed to be, he fought it tooth and nail but
it was time. Maggie had carried her family since age ten.... Enough was
enough! I think of the dog we had after Abbey. My little Dexie. A black-
and-white shiatzu with big old paws. He wasn't very liberal with his kisses
but when he was, it was something special. He was affectionate and had
eyes like saucers. Taking this dog for a walk was a trip. He would bark and
thrash like a maniac at anybody walking by. We felt blessed having him.
Unfortunately, we only had him for four years. He had a stroke.

I was going to group therapy for a couple of months. Things were
going well. The girl who animated and mediated was nothing short of a ca-
sually dressed goddess. One night Maggie picked me up and I knew something was wrong. When we got home Maggie burst into tears. I looked
down and saw Dexie sprawled on the floor. I immediately brought him to
bed and began stroking him. He started thrashing and crying, this was it.
As hard as it was to get over Abbey, Dexie was even harder. We only had
him for four years. He was sweet and loving. God bless you, boy, I'll miss
you.

Maggie's mother, from all I've heard, was the sweetest woman on
the planet and I believe it. I really wished I could have met her. She smoth-
ered Maggie with love, true. In the late eighties, Maggie had decided to go
on a trip to Europe...GREAT!! When Maggie was at the crossing through
the gate, her mother began crying and screamed out that she felt as if she
would never see her again. "DONT GO, MAGGIE!!" She was pounding
on the window like it was a bad movie. It turned out that while Maggie
was on vacation, her mother died. She had to come home and take care of
things. She recalled saying that on the plane ride home she wished the plane
would crash. That poor girl.

Now I was living with Maggie. Rose got her own little place. My
artwork was intense. Heavy paintings that no one would ever want.... Still

whenever I did one I felt ageless, timeless and nameless. The setup was always the same. I would be in my mother's unfinished basement. I would slip into something grungy and get my paints in order. Bring down my boombox and put my canvas on the ground. Put on *Ten* by Pearl Jam. Pound back maybe five beers and just let it flow!!! The music would just transport me into another sense of being. I wasn't myself but I was here!

I went to this apartment party on the South Shore. It was full of shady characters...most of them good friends dating way back. I was dressed in a B-Boy sweater with pants even though I was a rocker. PANTERA was playing, bringing up the testosterone levels. Still love PANTERA but what happened next was fucking ugly. I opened the door to the bathroom and there was a stone-faced Frank V. He pushed me. "Faggot!" he said. I pushed him back. Suddenly, John Le had me in a headlock. They both began pummelling me, "FUCKIN' FAGGOT!!!" Everyone just watched. Some people even laughed. I left covered in blood and shame. One time camping in New York State, my parents visited us. My father and I made a fire together. The rain started and we did our damndest but it just wasn't happening. We gave it our best. My parents took pity on us and let us stay at their hotel. It was nice sitting there all warm with a rum and Coke watching reports of hurricanes, all the while being dry and quite content. It was nice to be dry!

Bob - 2002

The weight of my depression kept on pulling at me. But now we were going to Florida with my parents. We did the beach every day. When we weren't at the beach, we were at the pool. Corona in hand, from lunch to supper. One night we went to Tony Roma's rib joint. They made it as though you were in Vegas but food wasn't that great. We were also sat next to table with a couple of screaming kids. When we asked to be moved, they obliged but seemed a little put out...HAH. One afternoon, my dad and I were pounding back beer after beer by the pool spying this super-hot chick when my mother came out and demanded my father take her to a mall. "Jesus Christ! I'm half drunk!" he pleaded. Nope, and off to the mall they went. I tried not to laugh when I saw how sunburnt he was. Those days at the beach were majestic, lying in the sand, not worrying about anything but skin cancer. I would sneak a few beers to the beach and pound them back when nobody was around. "You'll watch our stuff?!?" Glug, glug, glug. My dad and I went down to the CVS for a female-related purchase. Dad went in but I stayed outside smoking a cigarette. This beautiful dark-haired girl kept looking at me smiling. She had an incredible body. To be honest, she was probably like seventeen. I didn't care. My ego was on flames. When we got back to the room I looked in the mirror. Oh my God! I was red like a lobster! I wondered if that was why she was smiling. SIGH! I guess I'll never know. Also, at the motel were some shady characters, the kind that maybe might hop a freight train. There must have been some been some kind of program but hey, do it somewhere else.

2003

This was the year Maggie's father died. I loved him. He was always nice to me. We had a special connection. Sometimes we would take him in his wheelchair to the adjacent park for a stroll. Maggie would always bring a few Coronas and we would sit there basking in the sun, enjoying our beer. He could never finish his beer so he would smile at me and I would do the honors. Sometimes I wasn't sure what he was saying so I would just say, "SI!" There was one time, a day or two before he died, when I looked deep in his eyes and when I did his eyes grew wide. I had never seen anything like it. As if I was death. Maybe I was. Maybe I should look in the mirror. I miss him to this day. I remember when we first met, I called him Hose B instead of Jose. Not long after, Maggie said that her father asked her why I continually called him roast beef. That deserves an LOL.

2004

The worst boss I ever had! He was really macho, a black man, which he always reminded us of. Also an unabashed racist. I can remember him calling Prince a half-breed. Fucking PRINCE!! I was very hypervigilant as to what was said. It didn't matter...Asian...bipolar...trans...HE was a bully with me but not with the other guy we worked with.... THEY WERE "BROS"! I can only hope that this guy got what was coming to him after being bullied for three years.

2005

I was functioning just fine but would need it to be over. I would continually think of a plane crash or maybe the bridge collapsing. My genitals and tongue being sliced by a printing press. I call these razor thoughts and I had to live with them all the time. I soon changed my medication, it was not a huge difference from the medication I was already taking. It strengthened my mental armor at work. I hoped it wasn't just a two-week manic high followed by a physiological nosedive.

2006

My father looked a lot thinner. He would speak in riddles. Not that he was demented, just heavy. He was sick, lung cancer. I was the last to know. When I realized I broke up hard. Thinking of him driving to the country place with me standing behind him, I felt so sad. He kept quoting a song, "Nothing I Can Do About It Now," by Willie Nelson. He never wanted to stop working either. Someone had to tell him to stop coming in. One afternoon I was watching over my dad. He was quiet. Then he sat up and said, "I want to go!!" I thought that he wanted to die and I couldn't blame him. He said it again, this time pointing to the bathroom. Oh, man, he wanted to go to the bathroom. I sheepishly obliged. Fred told me once that he was never ashamed of me, that was enough for me. Have to say, he never changed who he was through the sickness, like how he always hated loud noises. One night a nurse had let a door slam. It was pretty loud. "Sorry," she offered.

"NO, YOU'RE NOT!" my dad replied. My sisters and I took turns staying with him overnight, making sure he was okay, squeezing his skeletal hand. I'm sure our whispers of "It's going to be okay!" got to him after a while. You just don't know what to say sometimes. He was never a huge guy, just one of those guys you don't fuck with.

I was working on a big job the day my father passed. At one P.M. that day, Maggie burst into the mailroom, tear laden, saying my father had died. "We're going to go see him," she said. I knew my dad had had an impeccable work ethic. I would finish this job for him. Maggie would pick me up later. When she did pick me up the weather was like death. My body felt the exhumation of right then and there. At his funeral, we all rose when they played that swan song, "Nothing I Can Do About It Now." I liked that it wasn't your typical funeral fare. It was a straight-up country song, nothing against Sarah McLaughlin but this was perfect. Religious shit was kept to a minimum. My dad was an atheist...well done. As my father was being lowered into the ground, I remember wishing he knew me better. Way back in the eighties being bipolar was not really understood.

One night, I was laying on my side when I heard a metallic roaring sound. Suddenly a yellowish tarnished face with sharp teeth appeared a centimeter away from mine. I found that hard to deal with. Also when I get overwhelmed, sleep is hard to come by. Sometimes I understand movies. That's when keeping my eyes open is too intense and when I close them I see reels of hard and disgusting footage.

Thus spate the karaoke man. Maggie's brother had loaned us a karaoke machine. I immediately began ordering karaoke CDs. They gathered fast, from Johnny Cash to Slipknot. I had everything. It wasn't enough, though, I had to do it live! We found a place in Gatineau...the GAT, I called it. I went on stage and sang a Guns & Roses song to a wild response...high-fives and hugs. It was GREAT. There were many home shows that were not seamless. I may have displayed an AXL-like behavior at times. People would be aghast. I did not rehearse for days but for months. I tried not to look at screen for guidance but more to make like a real performance. It brought me back to singing AC/DC in the mirror as a kid. I knew I would rock someday. This was someday. A karaoke performance every few months. One special karaoke performance I did in drag..."Poker Face" by Lady Gaga. I got all dolled up and a little slutty! It was great. I guess everyone has a male and female inside. I was one hot bitch!!! I borrowed a dress from Maggie. I just had fun and let loose. I knew there was gossip in school that I was GAY.... Here you go, motherfuckers!

2010

Victoriaville, Quebec...
There was a Patton show starting in two hours. We had gone to the local

restaurant near the venue. We had a nice meal with a pitcher of beer. As we were eating, I said to Maggie, "Hey, wouldn't it be funny if Patton were to walk in?" I couldn't believe it but Mike Patton and his bandmates walked in just as I said that. The name of the band was ZU and they were Italian. I couldn`t believe my luck. Maggie walked out on the spot. So I knew I had to get to Patton before their food came. I had heard some bad stories of him when he was bothered by fans while he ate. I approached his table and told them my name. The band members looked at me with disdain. Then I said to Patton, "Give me a couple of your favorite singers."

He said, "Dance Dickinson and Betty Boop."

Okay, so he was being playful, I wasn't. I said, "Some of mine are Rob Halford and George June."

He cocked his head, smiled and said, "Same page!"

I was happy.

Bucky

One of my closest friends I ever had. He moved away to the U.S. when we were in our twenties. We stayed in touch via email. One day, he texted me that he was not well. I instantly reached out to him. Worried, I told him that he could stay with us until he got better. He took us up on our offer. Everything was great at first. We had a lot in common, he liked the same music and television as I did. We never charged him room and board. But then I found out about his "Amor." He was using the money he would have had to pay for room and board to get his Amor from Chile into the country. Fuck you, buddy!

Maggie couldn't say no. His little relationship with Amor fizzled out after a few months but not before he sucked the life and money from us. Our internet bill skyrocketed because he was streaming movies from the U.S. but never did he offer to chip in to pay the bill. Instead, he bought himself a new SUV. He came home one night before supper and asked us, "Would you guys mind if I invited my new girlfriend over for a movie?"

It was the last straw! I said, "Sure, if you start paying rent and back rent?!?"

He hung his head low. Two weeks later he was gone. He found himself a new apartment. Two months later he left Montreal and went back to Pennsylvania.

Hey, Lady

My Britney was pretty good, ending with. A Nirvana song that left me screeching and howling on the floor, making everyone uncomfortable. Maggie had called me Axl Rose many times. She would ask me to turn down the sound on the karaoke player and I would slam my microphone down and start swearing or I had a problem with my wardrobe, either way I was a total diva!!! Kicking things off, my drinking was out of control but I found a new group that really helped. The woman who animated the meetings was nothing short of amazing...short, cute short blonde hair, but the way she got the group talking and participating, just incredible. I really curbed my drinking at this point. I did so well, in fact, that she told me I was doing fine and didn't need to attend anymore. She was wrong. I must admit, though, I had a little crush.

The Long, Hard Road into Hell

I awoke one morning with the thought of suicide in mind. This couldn't be good. And it wasn't. It was my standard "feel good want to end it" feeling, right there. Then I would cry and after another week back on track. Still, could I do it...end it? Whatever anyone tells you, it takes guts. I don't know if I have it. I know the impact it would have on friends and family. But I just can't seem to care. Suppose if I didn't have memories of a cock in my young mouth that I can't get out of my mind. Or permanently being the odd boy out, never feeling a part of school. Feeling like a lame duck at work. Where is the off switch? Close. That was what Maggie and I were not. At home we got on like an old couple. No sex. That equals no passion. And the question is this, "What do you do when masturbation has lost its charm?" You panic. You have fights that end in "I'm done, bitch!!" And yet I still loved her. Even though something huge was missing and something was about to change. But I did not want to leave her. I loved her still. We would occasionally cuddle. Therein lies the conundrum.

The music blared from the jukebox. Faith No More, one of mine. MAD HATTERS PUB, kind of dive but not so bad. I had already ordered a pitcher of Molson for myself when Tom arrived, a nice guy. He just couldn't look at you to save his life. Then super-manic Henry showed, John (Sheldon) not much later. So far we had a good crew. And then in walked my old friend "The Boy" and his "girl," as they shall be referred to. The girl and I got on like a house on fire. We had a fantastic night. I got a call from the boy on Monday at work. It felt weird like when a boyhood friend invited you to stay over but you were really not ready. But we were really reconnecting. He invited me to his place a week later. I was ready. Once I arrived at the Joliette metro station I was there. We drank like we never drank before. He lived in a basement apartment with the girl. The place was disheveled, clothes all over the place, beer cans littered every possible surface, overflowing crusty dishes. The boy was smoking bowls of pot. I knew he'd be out soon. The girl was even, pretty as well. 1:30 A.M., the ginger also known as the boy was out. The girl and I sat at the kitchen table talking...pretty eyes, golden locks, pouty lips and an hourglass figure....As we spoke, I could feel my body react to her. I couldn't take it anymore, I kissed her. It was nothing short of electrifying. Our kisses electrified each other. I stroked her cheek and we traded tongues. I kissed her neck.... "Ooooh," she moaned.... Now my hands were down her pants.... "Go check on him," she said. Yup, fast asleep. Suddenly, the girl was bent over, revealing her big white ass. I took my chance and dropped my trousers and all. I squeezed her ample ass and began pounding her. *My God, I haven't had sex like this in years*, I thought. This went on for a while until I realized that I couldn't perform anymore. I must have had at least sixteen beers total. I kissed her and apologized. She understood. The next day when I was leaving I passed her on the bed, she cocked her head and said, "I guess last night meant nothing?" I kissed her and assured her that it meant everything. I had crossed the line.

Right after that, I developed a chronic stomach problem. Along with my grinding depression, it was too much to bear. I picked up some sleeping pills and poked back half a bottle of rum along with a shitload of beer. I was dead inside. But by some miracle I got out of bed and hit my head on the bureau. Maggie called an ambulance. The ETM asked me, "Did you try to kill yourself, Mister?" "Mmmhhhnmff," I mumbled. "Okay, we will take you anyways, Mister." At the hospital, they treated me like another drunk. I fucked it up! Fast forward to a nice summer day, the boy had gone to the store, I immediately had my hands down her stretchy black pants. I deftly slid two fingers deep inside her wet pussy. She shivered and gasped until I had to stop...ahhhh! We began meeting for lunch on a regular basis. No eating, just kissing and squeezing. She wanted me to leave Maggie and she would leave the boy. She never stopped. "It felt like a Band-Aid being ripped off," she would quip. But she had nothing to lose and I had everything. Her texts would read like... "Well, my parents got divorced after being together for a long time...WHY CAN'T YOU?" On Canada Day, I brought the karaoke system over. We had a great time. I was amazing. I sang "VIVA LAS VEGAS." We raged and we snuck kisses here and there. The boy left once again. I took her by the hand and said, "Let's fuck." And I led her onto the front lawn and laid her down. It felt so good. I was now in love...again.

Now

Now she knew I wasn't going to leave Maggie. We began to argue about it. We went to a Weezer concert together and she went down on me as Weezer rocked the house! We went to supper as well. Still I knew she didn't love me anymore. It was never the same after that. We would kiss sometimes but she no longer was in love with me. She told me so. But I longed for her love. I'd go to bed so sad, thinking of ways to win her over. It took me a long time to accept it. Now and then she would send me a safe text. That was it. "What is it?" It was it, Maggie was the one I loved. I knew we had our problems. Who cares. I LOVE MAGGIE, non-refundable.

Downtown Karaoke

I was at a downtown karaoke bar with the boy and the girl. It was a section of the city I knew nothing about. I had had at least ten beers by the time we arrived. The girl would clasp my hand and kiss me when the boy went to the bathroom. Some girl came around to take our song orders. I would be the only one singing that night. I chose to sing "Enter Sandman" by Metallica. I ordered a pitcher of beer. I felt a drunkenness like never before. I went to do my song with a massive clapping response. When I meandered back to the table my friends were gone. I could barely stand on my own. I walked outside not knowing where the hell I was. I slipped on the icy sidewalk and landed on my face. I blacked out. When I came to, I was in a car with an older sleazy guy. I couldn't talk. I blacked out again and woke up in a hospital. I was definitely not going to stay. I quietly collected my clothes and walked out of the hospital. I took a cab to the boy's house. I began knocking on the window hoping he would answer. I gave up. I went walking down to the metro station, where I could find some warmth. It was so cold I was shivering nonstop. I had to wait till the metro opened. I should have called off our friendship for abandoning me like that. Things would have turned out better.

Gone

Once the pandemic hit my job changed and I hated it. So every Friday at lunch I would buy five beers at lunch and stealthily make it last the afternoon. It went like this for a year until I was called into a boardroom: "We had to let someone go and it's you. Sign these papers and you have a year's severance." "But we're family!" I sobbed. They followed me to my locker and it was humiliating. Twenty-eight years and I get this? I've drank every day since then because nobody really wants to die.

Epilogue

I've shook, I've shuddered, I've made the best of my time off. But there is always the inevitable. I could easily take my life or not. Rally in the last inning or not. I tend to think I'll rise up. This has been such a hard road. I've endured bullies, unsympathetic family members (except my mom...love you), some real-down disgustingly horrible bosses. You dig! I've made it this far and you can't kill me. Why let the thugs and pricks win? I have people who love me, who like me. Yeah! Let's all pick it up and go from here. CIAO!!!!!!!!!!!!!

Songs and Poems

Building

Now I don't know and I don't care, you are the stick, I am the snare
Making dark plans couldn't be any worse, all the days building up...
They say how you live is how you die but in God's name did they say why?
I'll leave you to rest and I'll carve out your sleep.
Your face is beautiful and I am a creep.
Making dark plans couldn't be any worse...all the days building up

Seasons

To every season, burn, burn, burn.
There is no reason, burn, burn, burnt.
And I can tell you I'm in hell and I can feel it raining down in heaven.
A time to get laid, a time to mourn, a time for a vision, no time for porn.
Swear it's not too late.

Change

Anytime I've wondered, anytime I've looked ahead.
You should call my uncle up, the chances are that I am dead.
I really just want you to see me, to see that something else
To see I'm something else.
Now you know I've always loved you.
Nothing takes away from that.
My libido is a little big, my belly is a little fat.
I really just want you to see me, to see that I'm something else
To see I'm something else

Day Drinker's Blues

I've got the blues. I've got the day drinker's blues
28 years, no job but you know I got booze
I woke up at eleven, then I put on a shirt.
People tell me I'm great but I feel like dirt.
I got the blues, I got the day drinker's blues
My girl, she understands me but after a while, "That's it," she said.
Baby, you been drinking two months, oh, now I think it's time to quit!
I've got the blues, I've got the day drinking blues

Work!

Hopeless pessimist!
Get the fuck dressed!
Time to erase the pain!
Be gloriously insane!
If I was me and you could see, I'd say it was over
I'd say...destined for glory.
Now you know the story, clouds making love, I see it from above.
If I was me and you could see, I'd say it's over
I'd say...say

Last Night

I fumbled through my thoughts thinking about last night.
A night that never did exist.
I met you at the bar, where we softly coexisted.
There is no use, we should be together
There is a strong, strong feeling.
Admittedly, I'm fucking reeling.
I'll let you govern the love.
I know that fate comes from above

I Wrote a Song

I wrote a song called KILL DEATH DIE
Wonder why I did it and I wonder why.
A seventh heaven and an intervention.
Well, at least, baby, I got your attention!!
KILL DEATH DIE...KILL DEATH DIE...KILL DEATH DIE!!!!!
I'm overwhelmed and I'm saturated
Synaptic response has been vacated.
I love your pussy and I love your tits.
I'll play the underground and you can play the HITS!!
KILL DEATH DIE...KILL DEATH DIE!!

My Annihilator

My annihilator. Long time coming, you asked for fifty-fifty.
My razor thoughts are through and I think that I am too.
My annihilator, my sweet love affair, it broke up and that's not fair.
Sweet little baby, I love you so much. I love when you watch old movies
and such.
In the beginning you hit my gut, then to follow I became your mutt.
My annihilator, my sweet love affair, it broke up and that's not fair.

Witchenol

Witchenol, the substance, it makes you feel this way
Witchenol, the Periodic Table, it feels it's here to stay
Witchenol, my liege, shields me when I'm under siege.
Witchenol, think I'll love you to the end even though you're killing me.
Witchenol, my liege, shields me when I'm under siege.
Witchenol, my friend.

Hold On to Heaven

2021, Captain's log.
Love your sweet soul, I love a sloppy kiss from a dog....
I keep on trying to reason but your voice was treason.
My heart is set on you, for sure.
Your sparkling eyes, my God, the allure.
I keep on trying to find the reason but your voice was treason.
HOLD ON TO HEAVEN
HOLD ON TO HEAVEN
HOLD ON....

Taste of Death…

Hey, Hey, Hey

All these years, how could I know thinking about hell below?
Taste of Death. Don't feel the pain anymore that I get the more that I gain.
Taste of Death.
The talk of death drives me out of my mind so much that I want to live.

Smart 514

Remnants, that's what I'm seeing...debris!
Hail the light, I'm killing it in the name of God!!
Fuck you good like a hot rod, SMART 514.
I have never been able to play.
I want my first kiss and everything else that goes along with it.
I'll give anything...
I guess it's just remnants

Only

You've only start living once you want to die
The truth is universal. The answer, I don't know why!
Wrecking it all, my health and all.
I'm sorry, babe, I didn`t do it hurt to you
The truth is universal, the answer is...I don't know!

Dirrrrty

And now I'm dirty and don't care!!!
My parents took me to the Brome fair
Flame hurt lie, love why?
Now I'm wasted, I'm in a trap, like chocolate, melted bliss.
Turn around and gimme a kiss
Flame hurt lie, love why!!!!

Lemon

You're as sweet as a lemon and I'll take it to heart.
My sweet vivisection knew from the start
Need you to love me.
Want you to love me.
My only request is that you heal me.
Love you always.
Can you feel me?
I won't move ahead without permission.
I'm lying in bed giving out transmissions.
Be next to me, love me

True

Hey, and what I thought was true, you do you and maybe I'll do you....
I've never burned with such intensity
Like I was on fire in one city.
I love you like diamonds and you have no use for them.
And still I love you.
I'll continue loving you, yeah!
Continue praying, yeah!
I still love you and that's no lie
Don't hurt myself and say why?

Maggie

I feel the sadness wash over me like a dirty brown wave.
It's official, vacation is ruined.
All the things I owed you, all the things I stole from you.
It causes a condition. It always leaves me wishing that you could see me.
See me as I am.
I am as you see me.
I see that you love me...forever

Darkest Dread

Darkest dread. Dread is dead.
But I've got a feeling, set your mind reeling.
A real long shot but worth it.
It's better than feeling like shit.
What if we all could smile?
One thing I'll say that you gotta believe.
Learn to be happy and learn when to leave.

Hard

I love you now.
Hey, even how you're a walking sex show
He said tell me something I don't know
I'd give up my own breath.
If you knew, my dear, I would love you to death.
My happy hours just cuddling you.
I'll hug you so hard, our past will not be marred.
Because at the end of the day, I love you hard.

Lightning!

I'm writing in lightning.
I'm dreaming in twos.
This world has me shaking.
And I've got the blues.
I'm dreaming I'm awake
Where's love, for heaven's sake?
I'm bending my limits, only God knows what's right.
I just wanna love you, I don't wanna fight.
I'm dreaming I'm awake, where's love, for heaven's sake?

Redemption!

I've never seen a firetruck drive so slowly.
I've never really bottomed out but feel so lowly.
I'm counting all my friends on just three fingers.
I had a funny dream and the taste still lingers.
Felt it all, my sweet addiction
Fuck it all beyond redemption.
I always really wanted to sing for my father
At this point I shouldn't even bother
He's gone now, passed away in the wind.
Probably mad for the way I have sinned.
Felt it all, my sweet addiction.
Fuck it all beyond redemption.

Mike Patton

I will never forget the first time I met my hero, Mike Patton. He had driven to Winooski, Vermont. Knowing that Patton and Rahzel, best beatboxer ever, would be there, I hurriedly got out of the car when we arrived. I could see him at the bar having a martini, classing it up! I had to meet him. I said to Maggie, "Let's go in!" She said a plain, emphatic "NO!" So I went to the ticket taker and asked if it would be possible to use the bathroom. I went in and saw Patton speaking to the club owner when I descended on him. "Hey, Mike!" I said nervously. "Hi, man!" he said. We began talking about Montreal and how he had a lot of friends there. I had to commemorate this moment with a picture so I pulled my camera out of my pocket. Maggie then took the picture for me. Then Patton said, "I love you, man. Now get the fuck out of here!" Beautiful!